AF264593

Inklings

Katherine Parry

Copyright © 2017 Katherine Parry
Artwork by Lisa Tangkai Schlossarek
All rights reserved. No part of this publication may
be used or reproduced in any form or by any
electronic or mechanical means, including
photocopying or recording, or by any information
storage and retrieval system, without prior written
consent from the author.
ISBN:9780473417543

DEDICATION

This book is meant to be held, loved, tear-
stained, drawn on and written in.
This book is for you.
It will be there for you through every
stormy night and every sun soaked morning.
I hope you find solace in its pages,
inspiration between the lines.

CONTENTS

Acknowledgments

ACKNOWLEDGMENTS

This is a thank you. An I love you. A cup of
tea on the counter and a key under the mat.
I am who I am because of you; this book
exists because of you. This is dedicated to
every person who has ever had belief in me,
read a piece of my writing or simply inspired
these words. Thank you for reminding me
of my strength and courage. For your
unwavering support.

Artwork is by the talented and beautiful Lisa
Tangkai Schlossarek. What an honour it is
to share these pages with you.

This book is dedicated to the Parrys. The
best people I know. We got there eventually.
I hope you are proud.

THE STORM

sometimes i don't know

if it's the neighbours slamming doors

or a storm raging outside

sometimes i think i wish the skies
were opening up

just so i could blame this feeling in my chest

on something other than my mind

the world won't stop spinning,
like that time you drank vodka and played on the
swings at the park. you swore you could touch the
sky, but maybe that was just your mind playing
tricks. it's always liked to do that.

like that time you sat in the cupboard in your
kitchen and cried into your folded arms. you silently
called it your sanctuary, until your shoulders
outgrew it and you found yourself crawling
underneath your bed frame for solace instead.

you can't see your reflection in shop windows
anymore. you only catch glimpses of a girl you once
knew as you walk past. her eyes shine a bit brighter
than the ones you stare at in the mirror every
morning.

you don't know when it happened, the moment you
lost your footing, or maybe you simply fell off the
edge. but you didn't ask for this. you didn't ask for
the shades of grey that have found a home beneath
your eyelids, or the salty tears you lick off your lips
each day.

the world won't stop spinning and you're just trying
so desperately to hold on to something you're not
so sure even exists anymore.

on days like these
i'm not sure my body can survive

give me something good
and i will tear it from its hinges
a hurricane within my ribcage
poison ivy beneath my skin

on days like these
i find it hard to love
my delicate hands and crooked jawbone
beneath the weight of this crumbling city

she said to me

"you've got pieces missing"

as if i didn't already know
as if i hadn't already tried to sew myself together
time and time again
she said that i've got pieces missing
as if they can be found again
but what if they never existed in the first place

what if this is all there ever was

i'm just trying to live.
to be honest with you.

sometimes it's hard. sometimes it's hard to love
somebody an ocean away. sometimes it's hard to
get up in the morning and tie my shoelaces.
sometimes i sit in the shower and cry. sometimes i
lie on my bedroom floor. sometimes i walk through
alleyways by myself at midnight. i'm not so sure
why. i'm trying to live. the best i can.

i swear

you were a child the first time your mind ran away
from you. you've been searching ever since.

sometimes your hands twitch and your skin doesn't
feel like your own. there are only so many times you
can claw at your own neck. you've become more
familiar with the 3am darkness than the sunlight
your friends try so desperately to grasp.

some nights, you're not so sure this even exists.
you'd sell yourself to the devil if it meant freedom;
free of yourself, free of the monsters that call your
body home.

you say that you understand
but you couldn't possibly

not until you've sat beneath a flickering light
with demons crawling beneath your skin
whispering love songs into your ears
yelling to be heard

you couldn't possibly understand
until you've torn at your skin
at your hair
at the ground
begging for it to stop

it's not a game
it's not a fleeting moment
it's a sinking ship in the midst of a storm
it's a graveyard growing inside of your chest

i cannot fix you so please do not ask me to try.
i keep a box of pills in the drawer beside my bed
for the nights i have trouble sleeping. i have marks
on my skin to remind me of the times my body
tried to tear itself apart. sometimes i look in the
mirror and don't like the person i see.

please don't ask me to fix you, i'm having a hard
enough time trying to put my own pieces back
together. i will be here when your bones feel
broken and you cannot pick yourself up off the
bathroom floor. i will try my hardest to turn your
tears to stardust and bring colour back to your
cheekbones, but i will not save you. i can't.

the truth is
i find it hard to breathe
on more days than not
as if my lungs are a ticking time bomb

sometimes i walk through the darkness
wondering if i could just disappear
like footprints in a blizzard
like a boat in a storm

i don't remember
ever feeling anything else
but this hurricane within my chest
these flames beneath my skin

THE SUN

sometimes i feel
like the debris left after a hurricane
damaged and misplaced
but other times i feel
like the eye of the storm
reckless and powerful

when you're in the depths of it all
it can be hard to swim
as your arms begin to fail you
and your lungs run out of breath

it can feel like you are drinking
bottles full of rocks and thorns
losing yourself beneath tidal waves
and leaving remnants in the sand

but as your mother once told you
at six years old
every storm will end
and sunshine will saturate your face
like those characters
in your favourite film

you will be okay

people break
like bones, glass, porcelain plates
but that doesn't mean they're broken

you see
the japanese have an art called kintsugi
where they repair broken pottery with powdered
gold

it embodies the idea that something cracked
can be even more beautiful than before

it may sound romantic
to sew your wounds together with diamonds and
gold thread
but you will never quite mend the damaged

that is okay

healing is a never-ending process

but as many poets will tell you
their tongues dripping in hope
if a person doesn't have a few cracks and bruises
how is the light supposed to shine through?

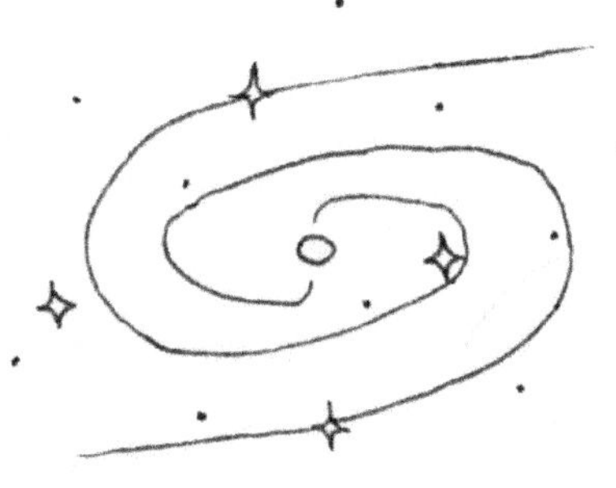

you think that you're broken just because they
threw rocks at you?

you think you're in pieces just because your body
tore itself apart?

oh, honey. stars explode from the inside. they self-
destruct to become supernovas. you have stardust
crawling in your veins and galaxies beating inside of
your chest. you can't destroy beauty, you cannot
dim a star. supernovas can outshine an entire
galaxy. flowers can grow in the toughest of terrain.

so tell me again that you're irrevocably damaged,
that you'll die before you ever shine again.

you matter
i hope you know that
as much as any constellation in the sky
or some obscure solar system
that nasa discovers
and celebrates in neon lights

you are alive. say it. soak it into your skin. you are alive. there is a garden of flowers growing in that graveyard in your chest. there is star dust in your veins and galaxies beneath your skin. did nobody ever tell you? those stars died so you could live. they breathe within you. stop looking up for heaven, stop waiting to be buried.

there is a fire behind your eyes and a twinkle you'll never quite catch. you twiddle your fingers when you're nervous. your hair never falls the way you want it to. sometimes you struggle to articulate the feeling that flows through your body. sometimes your lungs burn and your knees collapse and you become a prisoner to your own self-doubt. but, you are alive. nobody ever asked for more. nobody ever expected you to tear yourself apart from the inside out. on those days you feel like a branch on a forest floor, know that you are more. you are mother nature and the fire that burns it to the ground. you are the ocean and the boats it swallows whole. you are everything. you are all you ever need to be.

you are alive.

you can cry gasoline and set fire to your skin but i
will still love you. unconditionally. you can throw
knives and speak with poison on your tongue but i
will still adore you. irrevocably. you can break your
bones but i will put them back together. endlessly. i
will hold you in the dark, stand back as you glisten
in the light. forever.

sometimes you might feel like you are not enough,
like your body is about to collapse under the weight
of your own self-doubt. but let me tell you a little
secret, you are more than. you are liquid gold
spilling out of a merchant's cup. i will not let you
feed yourself to the wolves. i will plant flowers of
love on your collarbones and watch you bloom.

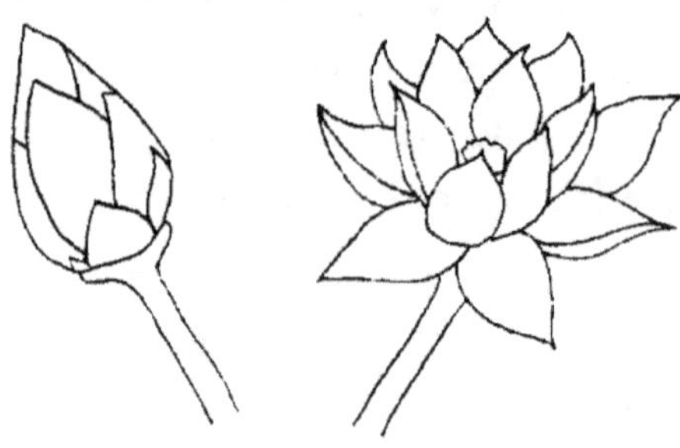

your worth is not measured by the
amount of hands that have touched you
or the amount of diamonds you own.
your worth is measured by the way your
eyes crinkle when you can't help a smile
and the way you bite your lip when you're nervous,
or the way you don't do either of those things.
it is the way you love and the way you lose.

your worth is measured in you being alive.
you are important simply because you exist.
you are a jigsaw and it is all your individual pieces
that make you worthy of kindness and adoration.

you will never quite know just how many times
you have been spoken of with love,
or how often the stars have been thanked
for your presence.

let me tell you something;
your worth is not a number on a scale
or a number in a bank. it is not your
mistakes or the pieces you try so
desperately to hide.

it is the gold that radiates from
beneath your skin, the flowers that
bloom from your fingertips.

i guess you could say
that i forgave myself
a long time ago

accepted
that i won't be the prettiest
girl in the room

but it's okay
trust me
it is

because there are constellations in my eyes
somewhere between the trees
above a smile that can light up a room
and skin that mimics the strength beneath

so yes it is okay
that sometimes my rose tinted glasses fall
or my heart forgets its pride

because turns out
there's an entire list of beauty and excellence
mapped upon my face

i'm sorry
if sometimes
your shoe laces come undone
and you find yourself crying
on the floor of somebody else's shower
or that you stumble on your words
and write diary entries about the
mistakes that haunt you

just know
that flowers will always grow
even in the coldest of winters
and that there is an entire garden
flourishing within your bones

your chest is not a graveyard
and though at times
it may feel hard to breathe
the sun will continue to rise
and you will light up the night
like a burning wildfire

that's the thing about rock bottoms: you can't
possibly get lower, you can't possibly fall further.
until the floor starts crumbling and you find
yourself a thousand feet deeper. it's easy to look up
and lose all hope. it's easy to curl into a ball and
give up. it's easy to build a home within yourself
and decide that it's good enough. it's not. you
cannot wrap your arms around yourself and hide
from the stars. they will keep shining.
they shine for you.

there is no such thing as peace and quiet, when
you're waging a war with yourself.

honey, it's time to fight. it's time to stand up and
get yourself out of that hole. a million more have
done it before you; a million more will do it long
after you are gone. be that picture on the wall, be
that lion roaring in the distance. save yourself
darling, show them the way.

i don't remember the first time i decided that i wasn't
worthy. worthy of love, kindness, the life i was living.
i don't remember the first time i spat words of self-
hatred at a mirror or decided my body deserved to be
destroyed instead of cherished. i'm sure there was a
time, in which a garden grew inside of my chest,
flowers scattered through my veins. i'm sure there was
a time i saw myself through rose-tinted glasses.

maybe it's the world to blame, the kids who liked to
make the tough girl cry. if only they knew. maybe
they'd delight in it, maybe they'd feel ashamed. i wish
i could have told that girl that she is doing alright; that
she is worth more than words could ever articulate.
that the sparkle within her eyes doesn't just exist, that
she earned it all on her own. i wish i loved myself now
the same way i love her. i wish i could protect myself
the way i would her.

some days it feels like i'm picking away the only
beautiful parts that still exist. i'm not quite sure how
to stop. i'm trying, i swear. some days my vision
becomes blurred and it feels like i've fallen off the
side of a cliff. some days it gets bad again. i'm trying
to remind myself that i am worthy. that i am made of
the same stuff that girl i love so dearly was. that a few
extra cracks doesn't always make a building tumble. it
seems so foreign, so wrong, to even consider, that
maybe i love myself. that maybe i am worth it. that
maybe there is gold beneath my fingertips and
compassion on my tongue.

i don't remember the first time i decided that i
wasn't worthy, but i hope that someday
i will remember the last.

i am a wildfire
i will not apologise
for the trees i burn to the ground
or the bodies i leave behind

i am a wildfire
and i will be seen
heard
felt

i am a wildfire
i will rage

feel the fear
and do it anyway

words installed in me
as my legs quivered
and my mind ran away
from cliff edges
and unfamiliar faces

there's something
about growing up conquering mountains
that grows inside of you
like a field of daisies

an idea
that you can do anything
and everything

because when you struggle
to keep your beating heart at bay
just remember
that you are alive

so feel the fear
and do it anyway
because those will be the moments
that earn you your armour

surround yourself with people who can see the gold
that glistens from beneath your skin. who will lie
down with you on a cold kitchen floor. watch the
sunrise with people who understand that true
beauty doesn't need to be tweaked. fall in love with
yourself through the eyes of those who love you.

sometimes the forecast will say nothing but rain.
that doesn't mean you have to stop hoping for
sunshine. sometimes you will meet people who
smell like candyfloss and have a fire burning behind
their eyes. keep them close. watch them sparkle in
the light.

join them.

there will always be people telling you to be a little
more this, or a little less that. there will always be
bodies and faces who try to stifle you under some
illusion of being supportive and helpful. or maybe
they'll wear their greed on their sleeve without
apology or remorse. people are people and you
cannot decide what or who they are.
they will just be.

but you, now you, will be whatever you want to be.
you do not need to search for warmth in the arms
and mouths of other people. you have it radiating
from within that ribcage of yours. you do not need
to self-destruct to be beautiful. you do not need to
stare at the stars when their blood flows through
you. so, your hands tire from writing down your
dreams all day? so, your eyes feel weak sometimes
and you struggle to sleep? it is not these things that
define you. you are everything all at once.
a body of burning galaxies.

your heart is beating
and your lungs are full
and baby, you're perfect
just the way you are.

sometimes
your mind doesn't quite play fair
sometimes
it feels like you're cutting your own fringe
with blunt scissors and a crooked mirror

you've never been so good
at being alone
you've never been so fond of the dark

but
just because you can't feel something
doesn't mean it isn't there

you see
there are a thousand exploding galaxies
beneath your skin
and any moment
you feel like your lungs might cave in
know that star dust
is flowing through your veins

it is easy to sit here and tell you
how magical you truly are
that every story will pass
and caramel sunlight will saturate your face

it is easy to speak with golden tongues
and rainbow fingertips
but the truth is
everything you have ever needed
exists within that body of yours
and it will get better
i promise you that

every princess has a part in their story
where they trip over their own feet
but there's a throne waiting for you darling
when the timing is right

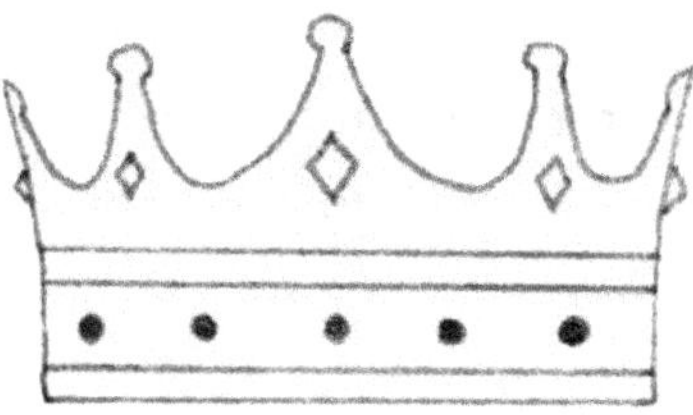

nobody ever told me
that i had the world in the palm of my hands
flowers growing from my fingertips
and galaxies exploding in my ribcage

nobody ever told me
that i could turn an ocean to stone
and tears to gold
with just one touch

i wish i had known
that there was beauty in my bones
and magic in my veins
before i tore myself into pieces
trying to make art
from something that already was

i may be fragile
with a delicate touch
but if you drop me i will not break
i will not fall apart in your hands
like that china plate your mother adored so much

sometimes my hands shake
and my voice quivers
i've never had the bravest mind
or the strongest knees

but if i slip from your grasp
i will not shatter
throw me to the ground
and i will stand up taller

this body is made of metal
rocks
a thousand exploding galaxies
you think you can break me?

baby
i'd like to see you try

it seems foreign to think
that maybe i deserve
the sunshine that i bask in every morning
or the rain that feeds the flowers
i take home for my mother

it feels so unnatural
to look in a mirror
and speak words of love
admiration
beauty

to delight in the lines
that crease on my face
when i can't help a smile

i'm not so sure
when i started setting fire to my bones
i'm not so sure
when i started burying
the goodness within me

it seems like a lie
to admit
that i am worth more
than other people's perceptions
that i am not defined
by the things i have been told
the behaviours i have learnt

perhaps the problem
doesn't exist within me
but the mouths of others

we all just want to be loved
that's the silent truth
laid bare for all to dissect

we all just want to be appreciated
to know that we matter
that the atoms that make up our body
aren't as insignificant as they seem

some of us have a steady grip
others shake as they try to open jars
we've never claimed to be perfect
to not bite our own tongue
or trip up flights of stairs

but sometimes the sun rises
and we feel less than
like the stardust beneath our skin
is simply dust and sand

we all just want to feel
like the feathers of a peacock
the first bloom of spring
like we're real
and important
and not just specks on an orbiting ball

i'm sorry if your mother never told you
that you are made of the most beautiful
constellations
that galaxies are growing
inside that chest of yours

i'm sorry if your father
didn't stick around long enough
to see you wed
or walk you down the aisle

i'm sorry that you cry on your bedroom floor
sometimes
and that the word family
can feel like an open wound

i'm sorry that you didn't get showered in the love
you deserve

i'm sorry that all you got
was dead and withered rose petals

but i hope you know
that i will pour my love into you like a fountain
if that's what it takes
to make you realise
just how magical you truly are

sometimes you break your own limbs
trying to prove that you don't care
that you are alright
that the face in the mirror isn't truly your own

sometimes you beg on your knees
to anyone who will listen
you pray to the night
and whisper words of forgiveness

only
your body is a fortress
and you don't owe your bones to anyone
you yell in apologies
because that's what they taught you to do

let it be known
that you are more
than you ever needed to be
a palace draped in liquid gold
a sea full of diamonds

some days i wake up
wishing i could be something other than
these skin and bones

but on different days
i wouldn't rather be anyone else
or rest my head on another body
because
with a laugh like a lullaby
and a mouth full of poetry
turns out there's nothing better
than this crystal maze i call my own

i'm not very good
at spotting the stardust within my veins
the galaxies beneath my skin
and so i lay under the stars
tracing constellations with my fingertips
forgetting for a moment
that those same pieces of art
are freckled beneath my eyes
scattered across my collarbone

it's always surreal
to have that moment
when you look in the mirror
and realise that you adore the face
staring at you

it seems
our entire lives
we are taught something different
tongues made of poison
and shapes that don't quite fit

i never thought
in my teenage skin
that i would find myself here
with my rose-tinted glasses
and delicate limbs
but with every thunderstorm
comes a new beginning
a moment to step back
and say

"wow
we made it kid"

eight months from now
you see a garden
scattered in blossom petals
and your favourite worn out bench

you see the ocean
and a being that refused to quit
as she sows her seeds
and fights the waves
with a strength
you need to witness

like the towns that rebuilt themselves
she will continue to rise

turns out
even in the harshest of moments
when your body isn't so sure
and your mind feels fragile
you will survive

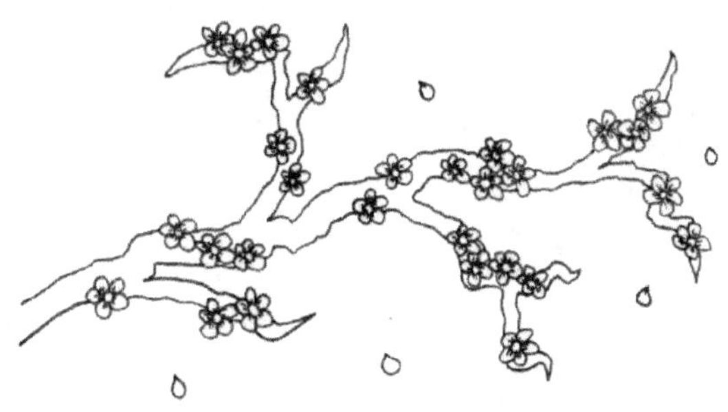

on those days when you feel
like a branch on a forest floor
remember that flowers can bloom
in the toughest of terrain
and cracks in the pavement

know that there are people
who fall in love
every time you laugh

who sit on rooftops and wish on satellites
mistaking them for stars
or maybe they just want to believe
that their dreams can come true
in the same way that technology orbits the earth

sometimes you might feel like not enough
like you're too insignificant

but know that there is beauty all around
that that same beauty exists within your ribcage
and even when your lungs burn
and your knees feel weak

you are alive

i stopped looking for a hero
inside of you

and found it
within myself

ABOUT THE AUTHOR

Katherine Parry is an England born, New Zealand
raised author. She spent her youth falling in love
with night skies and the way the ocean devours the
shore. She has lost and found herself too many
times to count. *Inklings* is her first book, stemmed
from a life lived with her heart on her sleeve.
Inspired by the wreckages that built her, this is a
story of love, self-discovery and what it means to
dance in the rain.

www.ingramcontent.com/pod-product-compliance
Lightning Source LLC
Chambersburg PA
CBHW061059050726
47592CB00004B/1739